The
Hill of
Enchantment

BOOKS BY RUSKIN BOND

Fiction

The Hoopoe on the Lawn: A Novel
The Night Has a Thousand Eyes: My Favourite Stories of Love, Warmth, and Friendship
The Gold Collection: The Master's Greatest Stories
The Last Tiger: My Favourite Animal Stories
Song of the Forest: Tales from Here, There, and Everywhere
The Shadow on the Wall: My Favourite Stories of Ghosts, Spirits, and Things that Go Bump in the Night
Miracle at Happy Bazaar: My Very Best Stories for Children
Rhododendrons in the Mist: My Favourite Tales of the Himalaya
A Gallery of Rascals: My Favourite Tales of Rogues, Rapscallions, and Ne'er-do-wells
Unhurried Tales: My Favourite Novellas
Small Towns, Big Stories
Upon an Old Wall Dreaming
A Gathering of Friends
Tales of Fosterganj
The Room on the Roof & Vagrants in the Valley
The Night Train at Deoli and Other Stories
Time Stops at Shamli and Other Stories
Our Trees Still Grow in Dehra
A Season of Ghosts
When Darkness Falls and Other Stories
A Flight of Pigeons
Delhi Is Not Far
A Face in the Dark and Other Hauntings
The Sensualist
A Handful of Nuts
Maharani
Secrets

Non-fiction

It's a Wonderful Life: Roads to Happiness
Rain in the Mountains
Scenes from a Writer's Life
Landour Days
Notes from a Small Room
The India I Love

Anthologies

A Town Called Dehra
Classic Ruskin Bond: Complete and Unabridged
Classic Ruskin Bond Volume 2: The Memoirs
Dust on the Mountain: Collected Stories
Friends in Small Places
Ghost Stories from the Raj
Great Stories for Children
Tales of the Open Road
The Essential Collection for Young Readers
Ruskin Bond's Book of Nature
Ruskin Bond's Book of Humour
The Writer on the Hill

Poetry

Hip-Hop Nature Boy & Other Poems
Ruskin Bond's Book of Verse

THE HILL OF ENCHANTMENT

~

THE STORY OF MY LIFE AS A WRITER

RUSKIN BOND

ALEPH BOOK COMPANY
An independent publishing firm
promoted by *Rupa Publications India*.

First published in India in 2024
by Aleph Book Company
7/16 Ansari Road, Daryaganj
New Delhi 110 002

Copyright © Ruskin Bond 2024
Illustrations by Apoorva Lalit
Photographs on pp. vii, viii © Bena Sareen

All rights reserved.

The author has asserted his moral rights.

The views and opinions expressed in this book are
those of the author and the facts are as reported by
him, which have been verified to the extent possible,
and the publishers are not in any way liable for the
same.

No part of this publication may be reproduced,
transmitted, or stored in a retrieval system, in any
form or by any means, without permission in writing
from Aleph Book Company.

ISBN: 978-81-19635-88-7

3 5 7 9 10 8 6 4 2

Printed in India.

This book is sold subject to the condition that it
shall not, by way of trade or otherwise, be lent,
resold, hired out, or otherwise circulated without the
publisher's prior consent in any form of binding or
cover other than that in which it is published.

*For my family,
and our cat, Mimi*

CONTENTS

Prologue: The Open Window / ix

PART ONE: My Life as a Writer / 1

PART TWO: Life Is Sweet, Brother / 77

Recommended Reading by Ruskin Bond /117

~

PROLOGUE

The Open Window

If a writer wishes to create a little magic with his pen he must find a little magic in his life. Magic is there if we look for it. And it can make writers of all of us.

I have only to open my window to see a magical world—clouds racing across the sky, mountains marching into the distance, the valley unfolding before me, the wind in the trees, an eagle high in the sky, and down below people on the move—friends, familiars, strangers.... And across the ravine Pari Tibba—Fairy Hill—and the lone pine tree where once I wrote a poem....

*And here I am, pretty ancient now, but still writing poems and tales and memoirs.
And this is the poem of all my days....*

PART ONE

My Life as a Writer

Chapter 1

While I was still at school, in the 1940s, the ballpoint pen was invented. The fountain pen was already in existence, but the cheaper ones were always leaking and messing up one's fingers. I preferred the old-fashioned quill pens which we were still using in class. The ink came in little pots which fitted into apertures on our desks. The ink on a page of an exercise book did not dry up immediately, and the blotting paper was a necessity. If you made a little ball out of blotting paper and dipped it in your ink-well, it made an effective missile. If the teacher was out of the classroom, ink-ball fights often took place, these missiles flying madly about the classroom.

I wrote my first story with a scratchy quill pen. If a quill pen was good enough for Dickens and Thackeray, it was good enough for me.

The first literary effort was achieved when I was twelve. It wasn't a story so much as a day-to-day account of the school's activities, with sidelights on friends, classmates, and teachers. It was, in fact, a journal—and a journal is something I have kept at various periods of my life.

That early journal filled up a couple of exercise books, but one day they disappeared from my desk—taken and probably flung away by a prankster, or even confiscated by a teacher. No matter. It was an early exercise in writing, but no great loss to literature. In those pre-plastic times the pages of exercise books made good paper bags.

∿

Boarding school doesn't give you much chance to be alone, by oneself, for any length of time. To keep boys out of trouble they are kept busy from morn to night—in the classroom, on the playing field, in chapel, or gymnasium. It's all about achieving eminence (on a Lilliputian scale), in sport or academics. No time for reflection and little time for reading. But the school library provided me with an escape route.

The Hill of Enchantment

Those who think there aren't many book readers around today would be surprised to know that there were even fewer circa 1950. In a class of twenty, there were only two who actually read any books—a German boy, Kasper Kirschner, who had spent the war years in a detention camp with his parents—and myself. In those days there was no TV, no internet, no multipurpose cell phones—none of the things we blame today for the lack of readers—but the love of books, of reading, of writing, was a rare gift indeed. There were comics, there was the cinema, there was dance music, but books? No. Reading required some effort, and schoolboys reserved their efforts for the playing field or the tuck shop or exits into town.

A kind housemaster gave me the keys to the library and told me I could use it whenever I liked. I held those keys for at least two terms—1949 and '50—and made full use of them. With their help, I could dodge morning PT, or extra classes, or—worst of all—bowling to the 'first eleven' batsmen in the nets, I'd secrete myself in the library and read or write a little, or just fall asleep in the armchair near the bay window.

It wasn't a big library, and not very representative, but there was enough to keep a young bookworm happy.

I feasted on the novels of J. B. Priestley, Hugh Walpole, Somerset Maugham, Graham Greene, and Compton Mackenzie, all big names at the time. The novels that left their mark on me were Priestley's *The Good Companions*, Walpole's *Fortitude*, Maugham's *The Moon and Sixpence*, Greene's *Stamboul Train*, and Mackenzie's *Carnival*—among many others. I was also enamoured of Conrad's shorter works and the plays of J. M. Barrie.

The reference section contained the complete plays of Shaw, Barrie, and, of course, Shakespeare. Shaw was clever but cynical and arrogant. Barrie was by then out of fashion (apart from *Peter Pan*) but I was charmed by the ethereal and tender quality of plays such as *Mary Rose*, *Dear Brutus*, and *A Kiss for Cinderella*. The Anglo-Saxon race derides sentimentality or any show of emotion, and as a result, Barrie is now looked upon as a literary curiosity. But reading his plays was a pleasurable experience.

I did not do much writing in that library, but it certainly set me on my long literary journey, during which I must have read some ten thousand books (purely for pleasure) and even written a few.

The Hill of Enchantment

A room of my own. That's what I always wanted.

When I was eight or nine, living with my father in New Delhi (1942–43), I had the entire flat to myself, because he went off to work in the mornings, returning only at five or six. Our khansama (cook) came during the day to make lunch for me—we called it tiffin—otherwise I was on my own, the nearest neighbours being our elderly landlord and his wife who lived at the other end of the bungalow on Atul Grove Lane. It was just a two-room flat, bedroom and sitting room, but I had made the sitting room my own, with a dartboard, a small bookshelf, a couple of board games (Snakes and Ladders!), and the old gramophone taking up most of the space.

Except when Daddy was at home that old gramophone was chief companion and friend. It had come with us from Jamnagar, and whenever I felt bored or lonely, I would wind it up, change the needle, and place a record on the turntable.

The record collection had grown over the years, and the records were packed flat in a couple of cardboard boxes. If they weren't kept flat, they warped in the heat and took on weird shapes and were unplayable. Those records were so familiar to me, that eighty years, later I can still remember most of the songs and the recording artistes.

> *Just like a sunflower*
> *After a sun shower,*
> *My inspiration is you!*
> *Just like the joy after*
> *Hearing a child's laughter,*
> *My inspiration is you.*

A song forgotten by everyone but me. And the singers were Layton and Johnstone, popular in their time.

And there was a wartime propaganda record, the words sung by the comedian Arthur Askey.

> *Adolf (meaning Hitler),*
> *You've bitten off*
> *Much more than you can chew....*
> *And we're going to hang up your washing*
> *On the Siegfried line*
> *To remind you of the red, white, and blue!*

Or words to that effect.

Daddy had joined the RAF at the outbreak of the war. Too old for active service, he had gone to work in the Codes and Cyphers unit. All very secret and mystifying. But when he came home in the evenings,

he would devote himself to his real passion, stamp collecting, and he had an extensive and valuable collection. He told me the stories behind the stamps, and that way I learnt a lot of history and geography. That good-looking boy king on the Iraqi postage stamp... one day he would be assassinated! Stamps told stories.

Daddy was subject to bouts of malaria, and during one severe attack he had to be admitted to the military hospital at Palam. I was on my own for a week, although our landlord Mr D'Souza, looked in from time to time to see if I was all right.

I spent about a week on my own in that flat. I did not sleep much on the first night. I kept the light on, reading *The Swiss Family Robinson* till about midnight. I recommend that classic for any boy or girl who has to spend a night on his or her own. If that family could deal with so many challenges and dangers, so could I! I put out the light and listened to the sounds of the night. Jackals howled. New Delhi was still surrounded by wilderness and a forested ridge, and the jackal population was formidable, outnumbering street dogs. Night birds called. In the room a mouse squeaked. No, it wasn't a mouse, it was a little half-blind shrew who shared the room with me. 'A chuchundar,' said the khansama when he saw it the next day. 'It's lucky. You will get money!'

He was right. When my father came home my pocket money was increased and so was the cook's pay. He made great chocolate puddings and fish cutlets. Like Jeeves, I believe that fish is good for the brain.

I had learnt to live alone in the dark, and since then I have never been afraid of the dark. I see the night as a friend. Sometimes I get up in the middle of the night and take a stroll up the road. The mountains beckon and the stars shine bright. Jackals slink away. Humans are abed. Except for a solitary drunk staggering home to a lonely bed or a hostile wife.

The middle of the night is a good time to write a poem or a rhyme or even a limerick. I enjoyed writing tongue-twisters, like this one, preserved over the years and improved upon from time to time: *slippery slippers skid and slide as I slink along the slimy sinuous slithery ship!* (You have to say it quickly!)

But at the age of eight, on Atul Grove Lane, I wasn't thinking of being a writer, I was busy making lists.

I was obsessed with making lists. Lists of all the films I had seen with my father, and their casts too. The cinemas of Connaught Place—the Plaza, the Odeon, the Rivoli, the Regal, were all familiar to me. At the Regal there was even the odd variety show, put on by American troops on recreational leave. There were bookshops and music shops, and my record collection increased. I made lists of songs and singers. I made lists of birds. And flowers. And trees. And books.

Was this making of lists of any use? I don't really know. Perhaps it helped to give me a tidy mind, enabled me to compartmentalize things as I grew older. And it helped to train my memory. If you give me the title of a well-known film made in the 1940s, I will give you its cast. And two or three years later, when I took charge of the school library, I was soon able to name any author and his (or her) major works without any difficulty.

But I never made lists of friends. If you make lists of friends you are in danger of losing them, a superstition I picked up along the way.

And I stopped making lists when I started writing stories. Because stories are about people, and people refuse to be listed or placed in categories.

∫

The Hill of Enchantment

I was lonely when my father died. I had lost my only companion. The news was broken to me by one of the teachers in my prep school—he said something about the good Lord needing my father more than I did, which I resented. What could the good Lord need my father for? Did he want his stamp collection? It took me years to reconcile myself to this loss.

They kept me in the school's small hospital for a few days, until I 'felt better'. There was no one else in the ward, and so I was left to my own thoughts and predilections. An ayah brought me my meals, and the school nurse looked in now and then, making valiant attempts to cheer me up. But the future, without my father, looked bleak.

When school closed for the winter break, I was sent to my mother and stepfather in Dehradun. I shared a bedroom with my small brother and two half-brothers. I had a small cupboard to myself, in which I kept my books and clothes. The gramophone had gone. So had my father's valuable stamp collection, appropriated by 'relatives' in Calcutta. My sister Ellen, a backward child, was to join us later.

I was used to being on my own, and I now felt the need for privacy. If there wasn't privacy in the house,

I would seek it outdoors.

Dehradun, in 1944, was a small town of 40,000 souls. (Today it is a city with a population of more than 10 lakhs.) In a few days of wandering I discovered almost all that there was to discover—the Paltan Bazaar, railway station, parade ground or maidan, cinemas (4), bookshops (2), schools (4), a few restaurants, the Survey of India estate, forest areas, leper colony, leper hospital, police stations (5), clock tower, mango groves, eucalyptus avenues, litchi orchards, tea estates (2), canals (2), dry watercourses, hotels (3), waterworks, main post office, small bakeries (several), fish market, sabzi mandi, schools, temples, churches, mosques. A spacious cantonment, Gorkha soldiers. A winding road to the hills.

I went (that is, I walked) everywhere, and saw everything, but I was never a part of anything. I was the outsider looking in. It was only when I got older that I finally went *in*—and discovered people.

All that I saw on these walkabouts must have been stored in my head because many years later these people and places reappeared in my stories. I have a good visual memory, and the past—especially those childhood years—comes back to me in the form of pictures. And

I stitch them together to make a story.

I made no friends on those long walks. No one bothered me. Occasionally one of the dhobi boys would call out 'Lal bandar!' (red monkey) but nothing worse. Still, it made friendly communication difficult. I was an Angrez, and the Quit India movement was in full swing! I kept to myself, avoiding crowds and the busier roads. I became used to my own company.

Cinema halls were places where I could retreat and escape into another world. Sitting there in the dark, oblivious to the presence of others in the theatre, I could dance with Gene Kelly or sing with Judy Garland or fall into a pond with Oliver Hardy or draw a gun even faster than Gary Cooper. And after the show I'd walk home in the dark, across the deserted parade ground, secure in the certainty that the dark was my friend.

Although, in my imagination, I could draw a gun faster than any gunfighter, I never liked guns, they stood for death and destruction. My stepfather, Mr Hari, was fond of 'shikar' and tried to persuade me to join him and my mother on their frequent excursions into the forests around Dehra. He was, in fact, a poacher, and these safaris usually took place at night. An animal—usually chital or sambar deer—would be caught in the headlights of his jeep and gunned down without hesitation. There were usually one or two fellow shikaris with him, and with all guns blazing they moved down whatever they encountered—deer or wild boar or sometimes a leopard. He was keen on shooting a tiger and hired a forest rest house for a week and took me along with him. He engaged a number of villagers to 'beat' the jungle, but the tiger stayed away and all he got was a junglefowl. That week in the jungle was very boring for me until I found an old bookshelf in the rest house, and then I was in heaven, lost in the world of P. G. Wodehouse, M. R. James, W. W. Jacobs, and others, while my stepfather and his friends tramped through the jungle cursing the absent tiger.

Sometimes books turn up in unlikely places, and in my humble experience a book hunt is more exciting than a tiger hunt—unless, of course, the tiger is hunting you!

Every year, when I came home for the winter holidays, I would find that we had a different home— or rather, rented bungalows or portions of a house— due, largely, to my stepfather's inability or reluctance to pay the rent on time. He neglected his car business, preferring to take his mechanics along with him on his many shikar trips. He forgot about income tax too!

And as for loans, they would be paid back some day....

However, in the winter of 1948–49, I came home to find that the bungalow was a fairly large one and that I finally had a room of my own. It was an old house, in need of repairs, and my room leaked badly whenever it rained. No matter. It was my own room and my own space and I was grateful for it.

I did a lot of reading that winter. One night, while a storm raged outside, I sat up till three in the morning, until I finished *Wuthering Heights*, a novel of great passion and atmosphere, a work that I have read many times over the years. There are some books of which we never tire, and this was one of them.

Very different was a humorous classic, *The Diary of a Nobody*, by George and Weedon Grossmith. I went through it in one sitting. I turn to it when feeling a little low or under the weather. It never fails to cheer me up. Mr Pooter, the diarist, is the ultimate in pompous confession.

I had already discovered Dickens at school. Now I read *Nicholas Nickleby*, *Sketches by Boz*, and *Barnaby Rudge*; three very contrasting Dickens novels. I'd found them in a cupboard in my grandmother's house, where they had been hiding for years, and I'd shamelessly appropriated them, along with *The Little Karoo* by Pauline Smith, a slim volume of short stories, beautifully written, about the travails of the Boers when they first settled in South Africa.

There appeared to be a South African connection in my mother's family. A large ostrich egg adorned the mantelpiece in the sitting room. Gerberas and zinnias, natives of South Africa, flourished in our garden, and there was talk of a legendary grey African parrot that had been part of the family for over forty years. Either Granny, or a great-grandmother had grown up in South Africa, but I never found out which, as I was too young to be interested in family history.

The room that leaked gave me the privacy I wanted. I had yet to start writing anything of note, and I had grown out of making lists. But I did a tremendous amount of reading that winter.

I have always read for pleasure rather than for instruction, but as the result of some crazy notion I gave myself the task of reading both the Bible and the *Complete Works of Shakespeare* in their entirety. My winter break lasted for three months and I accomplished this feat within this period. The Bible was easy. It's a compilation of great stories, written in wonderful but simple language, and I found myself copying the style of the King James Version in all its rolling cadences. Of course, I skipped all those genealogical tables. As a writer of lists, I should have put up with them! *Song of Solomon* was my favourite book in the Bible. Years later, when I read George Keyt's translation of Jayadeva's *Gita Govinda*, I found both books had one thing in common—a lyrical sensuality that ran through like a river in full flow.

I found some of Shakespeare's lesser-known plays rather boring, and couldn't help wondering if the same man had written all of them. The *Complete Works* included an unimaginative poem, 'The Rape of Lucrece'. Surely this wasn't the work of the same man who'd written *The Tempest* (my favourite play) and the sonnets.

So did I benefit in some way from all this committed reading?

It certainly helped me with my writing style and feeling for literature. Back in school I was to win the Anderson Essay Prize three years running, 1948–50. This feat is still recorded on my old school Bishop Cotton's honours boards. It meant something to me then, and still does. It marked me out as a writer, even as a schoolboy. You build on your early successes, learn from your failures; or try to!

But the discovery of literature wasn't my only discovery that winter.

Across the road from my room was the small canal that ran the length of the town. Walking along its banks I came to a spot where it went underground. A little further it emerged into the sunlight, and here I found a clump of maidenhair fern growing where the stonework met the earth of the bank. It was an enchanting sight, and I visited that spot every morning just to catch the glint of sunlight on the dripping fronds of this delicate fern—a fern that will flourish only where sun and water mingle in a steady drip or spray. A tender fern but with strong wiry stems, called maidenhair because the stems resemble a maiden's pubic hair—or so I read in a botanical book!

Books, lonely walks, a leaking room, and a fern, all combined to start me on a long literary journey.

Chapter 2

In December 1950 I did my School Certificate exam and came home no longer a schoolboy. I was sixteen.

Inevitably, we were in another house—the fifth in five years—and I was back in a common room with my small brother, sister, and two half-brothers. Instant rebellion. I threatened to sleep on the parade ground, or in the station waiting room, or in my stepfather's rundown Ford V-8, if I did not have some space to myself. Finally, after three weeks of harassment, my mother persuaded the landlord to let me occupy a tiny barsati on the roof of the main building.

The room was tiny, with just enough space for a bed, a desk, and a chair. But I had the broad, flat roof to myself; or rather, I shared it with crows, mynas, squirrels, and wild cats. I hired an old typewriter and settled down to the business of being a writer. There was nothing else I could become!

In a frenzy of creativity, I turned out articles, stories, and poems, and sent them off to all the newspapers and magazines in the country. Most of them came back with polite rejection slips; some probably went into the editor's wastepaper basket; a few went into my own wastepaper basket. My last resort was a little magazine in Madras (Chennai) called *My Magazine of India*, which published some of my skits and sketches and sent me money orders of ₹5 for each article. *My Magazine of India* survived on its ads for semi-precious stones, lucky rings and amulets, aphrodisiacs. There were astrological predictions; I read them! The literary contents were quite banal and harmless, as far as I can remember.

I valued those five-rupee payments. They were small, even for those times, but ₹5 enabled me to see three films, or buy two paperbacks or three magazines, or a good meal in a restaurant. It supplemented the five-rupee pocket money I received every month.

Then, after several months of trial and error, I sold a story to the *Illustrated Weekly of India*, the country's premier magazine. It was edited by an Irishman, C. R. Mandy, who was to publish many of my stories in

later years. This particular story was really a humorous sketch, a skit on a schoolmaster, and it appeared in August of that year, 1951. By then, I had made friends with most of the boys (and one or two girls) in our mohalla, my reclusive days being long gone. It was impossible to resist the friendly overtures of my young neighbours. I was to make many diverse friends in the course of that year.

The steps to my room—twenty-two of them, I remember—were fairly busy during the day, with the comings and goings of my newfound friends. They were not into books or literature—very few were in those days—and I suppose I was a bit of an oddity, banging away at the old typewriter or making up rhymes for their amusement. I helped two of the younger ones with their homework, and an older girl with her English lessons. I became a semi-official letter-writer, typing out applications for jobs, for leave from work, for absence from classes. I even penned a love letter for a despairing college student, but it did not work for him, she was in love with a Dilip Kumar look-alike.

The fifty rupees I received from the *Illustrated Weekly* for my story made me feel like a capitalist—the philanthropic kind—and I gave a small party on the roof. It was just a 'samosa' party, snacks and fizzy drinks, and there were plenty of leftovers for the crows and the cats.

After dark I had the roof to myself. Then I had complete solitude. Just the stars and the moon for company, and sometimes a few fireflies to light up the darkness. The room had no electricity, but I had a kerosene lamp and I would use it if I wanted to read or write. Apart from the articles and stories I was trying to sell, I was also keeping a diary, a private journal, and for this I wrote by hand in school exercise books. I wrote about myself but also about my friends and neighbours, describing the general tenor of life in our compound. I did not show it to anyone. A diary is a conversation with oneself and not for public consumption—at least, not in its pristine state.

In the hot weather, geckos (wall lizards) would seek shelter in my room, roaming the walls in search of mosquitos and other insects. Their tongues would dart out, seize the winged morsel, and gobble it up, much as a child gobbles popcorn. Sometimes a lizard fell on my bed or on some part of my anatomy. I had read an account of a South Indian treatise on wall lizards and the significance of just where a lizard fell. If it fell on your feet, you were going to travel. If it fell on your belly or buttocks, you were in for a love affair. If it fell on your forehead, you would be a great mathematician. And so on. But those lizards fell on me so often that I became quite confused as to their significance and gave up trying to find any meaning in them. But they were quite harmless, and scuttled away, not really interested in my future welfare.

I did not have a fan, so I left my door and window open at night, to allow the breeze (when there was a breeze) to cool the room. One night I was awakened by a hideous howling just near my bed. A jackal had found its way up my steps and was giving vent to its feelings. It fled when I returned its howl with a shout, but after that I kept the door closed at night.

And then the monsoon arrived, and the rain would come through the window and flood the room. But after the sapping heat of May and June those first monsoon showers were delightful. I would run out on the roof in my shorts to bathe in the cooling rain, and I would soon be joined by my friends—and sometimes *their* friends.

As the rains retreated my friendships flourished. But as the days grew shorter so did my days in Dehra.

Chapter 3

A monsoon downpour is preferable to an English drizzle.

That was one of life's lessons that I learnt when I left the lower Himalaya for the English Channel. A lonely beach can provide the solitude that a writer needs, but a beach crowded with summer tourists in various stages of undress is hardly inspiring. Still, Victor Hugo got something out of his exile in Guernsey—his study and desk are still on view there—and I did at least earn a living during my year and a half in the sister island of Jersey.

No room of my own. I had to share a bedroom with one of my cousins. But it was home for a time and I ought to feel grateful for it.

I went through three jobs during that period—once in a grocery store, then as an assistant to a travel agent, and finally as a clerk in the public health offices down near the docks. But I managed to do some writing—at night or on weekends—and typed out my little tales on a typewriter in the attic. Religiously, I sent them out to magazines, and, of course, they kept coming back, much to the amusement of my uncle, aunt, and cousins. But I had my old Dehra diaries, and it occurred to me that they might be turned into a book, something like Rumer Godden's *Rungli-Rungliot* or Denton Welch's *Maiden Voyage* or J. R. Ackerley's *Hindoo Holiday*—but different, of course, and mostly about coming of age in a small town in India. I started working on the diaries, rewriting them, giving them a storyline, inventing new characters, rounding out old ones, and expanding the narrative. After a few months, I discovered that I had written a novel! It was very imperfect, of course, but I was quite pleased with it and sent it off to a publisher. It came back. Off it went again, to another. Back it came. My relatives were delighted. They were witnessing a demonstration of sadomasochism. Polite regrets from Michael Joseph, Macmillan, Jonathan Cape. And then a letter—quite a long letter—from a certain Diana Athill, editor and junior partner with the new firm of André Deutsch. She loved the story, she loved the writing, but it needed a lot of revision if it were to be published.

Like a good boy I sat down to rewrite the entire novel. It was to be the first of three rewrites.

I'd had enough of Jersey and patronizing relatives. I'd saved about £20 from my salary. So, I threw up my job and made for London where, of course, I had to take up another job. I think I have a record of sorts for throwing up jobs; but they were easier to come by in those days.

I changed my lodging as often as I had changed jobs. From Belsize Park to Haverstock Hill to Tooting south of the Thames, and back to Swiss Cottage in North London, I was a restless soul; never able to settle down in a boarding-house existence.

It was an existence, not a life. Up at seven, make myself tea and toast. Rush off to the tube station. Office opens at nine-thirty. Three and a half hours of bookkeeping. Lunch break. Beans on toast at a nearby snack bar. Back to office. Another three and a half hours of dealing with pounds, shillings, and pence—other people's pounds, of course. Tube train again. Return to my room. Go out for a light supper. Return to my room. Write a little. Fall asleep.

Half Saturday and Sunday off. Go to the pictures. Walk about the town. See Diana Athill if she's free, inform her of progress on the book.

Solitude is something we seek, in order to stay in touch with ourselves. Loneliness is something that is thrust upon us, often as the result of pure chance. For me, London was the loneliest place in the world. I knew no one, apart from my would-be publishers, my landlady, and my co-workers in the office whose interests were far removed from mine.

I decided I would get to know London on foot. Sundays were spent exploring the East End, or tramping around Primrose Hill and Hampstead Heath, or visiting Kew Gardens at the other end of the city. I tried to discover the London of Dickens and Dr Johnson, the dockland of W. W. Jacobs, the haunts of Holmes and Watson. These landmarks were there to be seen. But, of course, the great city had changed over the years, and I could find no one who resembled a character from Dickens, or even P. G. Wodehouse, who wisely went to live in America after fooling us that there were people such as Jeeves and Bertie Wooster, the brainy butler and his empty-headed master.

I did not meet any well-known writers in London,

for the simple reason that I was still an 'unpublished' writer with no access to literary circles. But Diana Athill put me in touch with a producer at the BBC, and I gave a couple of talks about growing up in a changing India. They were done 'live', in a BBC studio, and I had to practise a bit beforehand in order to modulate the strong Anglo-Indian lilt in my voice. As a result, I sounded more like an excitable Welshman!

Those were radio days. Radio challenged the imagination. Television was still in its infancy and has never really lived up to its promise or expectations, but it's an effective vehicle for propaganda.

I had been in London for about a year when I began to notice some impairment of vision in my right eye. At first, I saw shifting spots. Then, after a few days, these coalesced into a cloud which obscured my vision. Fortunately, my left eye was unaffected. But as the cloud would not go away, I went to a doctor (on the National Health Service, then in its infancy) and he sent me to an eye specialist who had me admitted to the Hampstead General Hospital. I was there for a month while various tests and procedures were conducted, including an injection of cortisone (the new wonder drug) into my eye. The condition was diagnosed as Eales Disease. It had probably been brought on by malnutrition. I'd been living on baked beans and cheese toast and was beginning to look like a character in Orwell's *Down and Out in Paris and London*.

Eventually the eye problem cleared up and I was back to my usual routine. But London's damp and foggy climate did not suit me, physically or mentally. I was a child of blue skies and hot sunshine. I was still missing India—my friends, the foothills, the languid lifestyle of that year in my room on the roof…. And although my novel had finally been accepted by André Deutsch, it would be a year before it was finally published.

I was restless, itching to return to India. But would I be able to make a living there? I had no qualifications, no skills apart from my ability to put words together in an interesting way. I could write for magazines and newspapers and make a living of sorts that way. It would take time to write another novel. All I really wanted to do was *write*, but I was ready to put my hand to other things when the going got tough. I'd managed three different jobs in Jersey, another in London, and in none of them had I been 'fired'; I had always been left on my own.

And what had I gained from my sojourn in the West? I'd written a novel and found a publisher. I hadn't made much money but I always had enough to live on (a condition to which I would be accustomed in the coming years), and I had learnt to live on my own in a civilized albeit cold environment.

I wasn't leaving any friends behind, as I'd done when I left India. In my two years in London, I'd made friends with a few students of my age—a Vietnamese boy and girl, a quiet boy from Thailand—but they, too, were in transit, ready to go home when their studies were completed. They belonged to affluent families; they could study at leisure, if they studied at all.

No one would miss me if I went away. Absolutely no one. My latest landlady, a kind Jewish lady, was quite fond of me, but I would soon be replaced by another nice young man. My publisher–editor, Diana Athill, had gone out of her way to help me, but she was fifteen years my senior and had other attachments. Hopefully the book would come out someday!

On an impulse, I packed two suitcases, shoved my portable typewriter into a travelling bag kindly presented to me by my employers (who wished me well, but would soon replace me), withdrew my savings from the post

office, and made my way to the docks at Tilbury, where a steamer was ready to sail for Bombay (Mumbai).

It was the month of March, and the year was 1955. The other day I was rummaging through an old trunk when I came across my postal savings book with its last entry. I found I still have a balance of five shillings and nine pence. My contribution to the Her Majesty's (now His Majesty's) government.

Chapter 4

Dehradun, in 1955, was still a small town with a population of roughly 50,000 souls. I say souls instead of people because each person I knew or met was a distinct individual with a soul of his or her own. It has now become difficult to separate one individual from another (not just in Dehra) as people seem to have merged into a certain similarity, all interested in the same things. Or is this feeling of mine just an old man being a little disgruntled with the present? Friendship seemed to mean something then, or perhaps it was just that we had more time for each other.

The British had left India, but I felt confident that the English language wasn't going away. The *Illustrated Weekly* was still in the capable hands of C. R. Mandy. Most of my fiction appeared in that magazine. It was a productive period for me. Many of those stories still appear in collections and anthologies; 'The Night Train at Deoli', 'The Eyes Have It', 'The Woman on Platform Eight', 'The Thief', 'The Crooked Tree' (probably my favourite), 'Time Stops at Shamli'.... And when *The Room on the Roof* finally appeared, it was serialized in the *Illustrated Weekly*, with Mario de Miranda's evocative illustrations. (Mario de Miranda was an artist, cartoonist, and illustrator.) I was also writing for *The Statesman, Sport and Pastime, Shankar's Weekly, Sainik Samachar*—anyone who would publish me!

All this literary activity took place in two rooms above the Astley Hall shopping complex, then the social and commercial hub of Dehradun. Over the years, British names have been removed from roads, buildings, and institutions. Somehow Astley Hall never lost its name. And no one, till today, has the faintest idea of Astley's identity. Who was Astley? No one knows. Perhaps that was why his name has survived, although sometimes corrupted to Asli Haal.

I was without electricity throughout the two years I spent in those rooms. No light, and no fan during the months. My good landlady hadn't paid her electricity bills for several years, and the amount that was due was now beyond her means as well as mine. But there was a little balcony looking down on the busy road, and I could sit there in the evening and converse with my neighbour's cat. At night I used a kerosene lamp, and did most of my writing by its gentle glow. I wrote by hand, but in the morning I would type out my stories or articles.

It was good to be among old friends, and the old friends brought over new friends, and the new friends brought their friends, with the result that there were constant goings and comings during the day—a far cry from the lonely bed-sitting rooms of London.

So where did I find the solitude that I craved occasionally?

I found it in the busiest place in town—the railway station.

The station was a fifteen-minute bicycle ride from Astley Hall. When the urge took me, and when I was on my own, I would ride over to the station, park my bicycle outside, buy a platform ticket, and pass a blissful hour on a bench at the far end of the platform. No one paid any attention to me, people were too busy arriving or departing or looking for their children or their luggage. I sat there quietly and watched *them* as they went about their business. No wonder so many of

my early stories are set on trains or railway platforms. Spend an hour on a platform bench, watching the world go by, and you will soon have a story.

There were busy periods and quiet periods, and soon the vendors and some of the station staff got to know me, and I did not have to bother with a platform ticket. I was exempted from this formality, as were the coolies and stray dogs.

Over the years, I have known many railway stations. Old Delhi, where my Uncle Fred was the station superintendent from 1943–44. The little station at Barog, on the way to Shimla, where my father and I stopped for breakfast. Charing Cross station in London, where I sheltered on a foggy night, drinking endless cups of twice-brewed tea. Ambala junction, where as a schoolboy, I got lost. The little station in the jungle at Kansrao, on the way to Dehra, where only one train stopped in the middle of the night....

After I came to live in Mussoorie I saw less of trains and railway stations, but in my memory, I still hear the shunting of engines, the cries of porters and hawkers, the guard's whistle, passengers calling goodbye.... And suddenly the platform is empty and only a disgruntled-looking crow is sharing the bench with me.

Chapter 5

When I was twenty-three, I went to Delhi to stay with my mother, my stepfather, brothers, sisters, and several pet dogs (noisy Pomeranians) in the far-flung colony of Rajouri Garden. (They had moved to Delhi shortly before my return from England.) I hadn't been keeping well—irregular meals and poor food had resulted in chronic dysentery—and I was selfish enough to want some home cooking for a change.

While I was in Delhi, I was offered a job. I'd been freelancing for just over two years, and hadn't done too badly, but I'd spent all that I earned and I was afraid of running out of stories—I'd already written and published about forty, apart from short articles and sketches. The job offer came from CARE—an American relief organization, which had done good work in Europe after the war, and had now extended its activities to Asia. CARE India was a very small unit when I joined it. We were housed in a wartime barrack-like building in Connaught Place, and our chief was Oden Meeker, an intellectual, always courteous and encouraging, if slightly eccentric. After doing some routine work, I was put in charge of CARE's Tibetan relief program. It was July 1959, and the Dalai Lama and a few thousand of his followers had fled from the Chinese occupation of Tibet and sought refuge in India. My job was to visit all the refugee camps and centres, assess their needs, see what we could do to help, and put in my recommendations. So, it was only partly a desk job. I was often on the move, by train or by air, visiting these centres, most of them in our hill stations—Darjeeling, Dalhousie, Dharamsala, Shimla, Mussoorie—and in the forests of Bylakuppe, Mysore, where the warrior clan of Khampas had been resettled. Travelling a good deal, and then writing up reports and proposals meant that I could not do much of my own writing, but I kept my notebook handy, always ready to capture and preserve ideas for stories and articles.

I had some interesting experiences too.

In Darjeeling, I was staying in the same hotel as Satyajit Ray and his film crew, and witnessed the filming of a few scenes of *Kanchenjunga*. In Dalhousie I was mistaken for an American spy and followed by the local CID. In Dharamsala I had butter-tea with the Dalai Lama's sister. In Shimla I revisited my old school and had a glimpse of the goalposts which I had defended so diligently as a football goalkeeper. In Mussoorie, I found an empty cottage which I felt would suit me when I returned to freelance writing.

But it was three years before I could do that. Apart from the Tibetan relief program, there were field trips or other projects which took me to UP and the Punjab. I did some non-fiction—historical essays on some colourful European adventurers of the early nineteenth century—visited Sardhana, where George Thomas helped to train the Begum Samru's private army; Hansi, where James Skinner built up his own cavalry regiment; Aligarh, where the French general, De Boigne, trained Sindhia's Mahratta army; and other places associated with the freebooters who made the most of the anarchy that prevailed in northern India at that time. C. R. Mandy had retired from the *Illustrated Weekly*, and the new editor wasn't too keen on publishing fiction. So I gave him non-fiction. And in due course these pieces appeared in a slim volume called *Strange*

Men, Strange Places. It was but a brief departure from my preference for the short story or novella.

Solitude in New Delhi? That wasn't easy to find, even in the early 1960s. But across the road from Rajouri Garden, on the other side of the busy Najafgarh Road, fields stretched away to the horizon. I crossed the road and walked through the fields. Presently I came to a well. A camel was plodding round and round the well, drawing up water, watched over by a village boy playing on a flute. An idyllic pastoral scene. Nearby a flock of parrots settled in a lone babul tree. The boy was friendly and told me that the land and the camel and well were his father's. I remember that he had an extra thumb. He was quite proud of it. 'It should bring you luck,' I said.

On weekends, whenever I had time, I would visit the well and talk to the boy and his camel. The camel didn't say anything, it just kept circumnavigating that well. The parrots talked a lot.

Then I left Rajouri Garden and moved to Patel Nagar. Two years passed before I could visit the fields again. A lot can happen in two years. The fields had vanished. I couldn't find the well or the boy. New colonies had come up across the Najafgarh Road—

Punjabi Bagh, Tagore Garden.... What had happened to the boy? Perhaps his father had made a fortune from the sale of the land. Perhaps the boy had a sleek new car instead of a camel. That extra thumb had brought him luck. Or had it? I'd never know. In India, change can come about very quickly when big money is involved. But when change comes too quickly it can overturn the natural order of things.

Depressed by Delhi, tired of my job, anxious to get back to writing full time, I resolved to go to the hills.

'Who goes to the hills goes to his mother,' wrote Kipling, and although my mother and stepfather and family continued to live in Delhi, I resigned from CARE India (on the friendliest of terms) and took the high road to Mussoorie.

∫

I rented a small cottage on the outskirts of the hill station. The rent was only ₹400 per annum. Yes, per annum. Those were the days! The same cottage would fetch about ₹10,000 per *month* by today's standards, but in 1963, Mussoorie (and hill stations in general) were going through a slump. They had never quite recovered from the departure of their colonial clientele, and the Indian middle class had yet to become the prosperous force that it is today. Hotels were half-empty even during the 'season', and shopkeepers struggled to break even. Only the English-medium schools were prospering.

So I had this little cottage, Maplewood, to myself. Not only the cottage, but the trees around it, and the verdant hillside.

Although the cottage stood in a fairly isolated patch of forest, it was no Walden and I was no Thoreau. *Walden*, along with Richard Jefferies's *The Story of My Heart*, had been among my favourite books, and although at heart I was pagan, a nature worshipper, I did not attempt to emulate my heroes. For one thing, I was too lazy to try living off berries and wild honey. Collecting honey isn't easy, and berries can upset your stomach. I stuck to fried eggs and buttered toasts— two things I had learnt to make during my time in London. And besides, there were other people living on the hillside, interesting people, and they had stories to tell. And a little way up the hill was a school (Wynberg-Allen), and I was soon being visited by some of the good people who taught there. Friends from Delhi sometimes dropped in, and occasionally stayed a few days, so I was far from being a recluse. But I found time to write, especially in the morning when a pair of whistling thrushes heralded the dawn with their sweet duets.

I was eight years in Maplewood and it was one of the most creative periods. There I wrote *Angry River*, *The Blue Umbrella*, and *Panther's Moon*, and saw them published in the UK and elsewhere. There I wrote stories for *Blackwood's*, Britain's oldest (and most conservative) magazine, a venerable monthly for over 200 years, serializing Joseph Conrad's novels and the stories of Jack London and John Buchan. *Blackwood's* wouldn't survive into the twenty-first century, but it was good to be part of it during the final years.

There I wrote numerous essays for the *Christian Science Monitor*, a Boston newspaper that I had discovered just by chance. My rambles in the surrounding hills gave me plenty of material for nature essays and poems. The payments were modest, a hundred dollars for a thousand words—enough to keep in eggs and toast.

And I was still doing the occasional story for the *Illustrated Weekly* (now edited by Khushwant Singh) and other papers. Altogether, the late 1960s and early '70s were a most productive and fulfilling period. I was absorbing the atmosphere of hill and forest, and capturing some of their magic—and hopefully passing it on.

∫

At the bottom of the hill was a small stream and rising above it was a hill called Pari Tibba—Fairy Hill. From my window at night, I sometimes saw little green lights moving around on Pari Tibba. Fairies! Nonsense, said one of my neighbours. 'Just a trick of the light or a villager's lantern.' But I preferred to think of the lights as fairies, dancing and making love under the stars. On a knoll facing Pari Tibba I found a grassy spot under a lone pine tree, and sometimes I would sit there with my notebook and write the odd poem or a passage for one of my essays. I called it my Place of Power. No one else knew about it. I would spend an hour or two there, on alternate days.

Pari Tibba gave me several stories, including 'The Wind on Haunted Hill', 'On Fairy Hill', and 'Listen to the Wind'. The cottage gave me 'Cherry Tree', 'A Prospect of Flowers', 'Love Is a Sad Song', and 'Binya Passes By'.

And then, in the early 1970s, along came Prem and his family.

Prem came to work for me in 1971. He married a year later, and in 1973 his wife and baby son Rakesh came from their distant and remote village. The little infant boy won my heart, and today, fifty years later, Rakesh and his grown-up children form the nucleus of my adopted family, held together by the loving hand of their mother, Beena Devi. It's a long story, a saga in fact, and I cannot do justice to it in this short memoir, which concerns my literary life. But, of course, my literary and personal life are closely knit, and the personal often finds its way into my writing.... And so you will meet every one of them, sooner or later, in fiction or essay or memoir; sometimes even in a poem—'I was the wind last night....'

But to return to the thirty-five-year-old author still trying to establish himself and earn a few rupees, dollars, or pounds, the process was made easier for some time by an offer from a gentleman called R. V. Pandit, to edit his magazine *Imprint*, while he was in exile in Hong Kong. Mr Pandit had been extremely critical of the government of Indira Gandhi, and when in 1975, she declared an Emergency, many journalists as well as her political opponents were rounded up and kept in custody. Mr Pandit owned a restaurant and news

The Hill of Enchantment

magazine in Hong Kong; he thought it wise to stay there. *Imprint* continued to be published from Bombay, and my job was to collect suitable material (i.e., writers) for the magazine.

I worked from home in Mussoorie, and was able to keep the magazine going for the three and a half years I was associated with it. I'm afraid I could do little to increase its circulation, which kept dipping, but I did at least have the satisfaction of showcasing the writings of many gifted writers: the sporting stories of Moti Nandi (from Bengali), the stories of Krishan Chander (from the Hindi and Urdu), Bhishan Sahni (from Hindi), and fiction and poetry by Manoj Das, Kamala Das, Nergis Dalal, Keki N. Daruwalla, and others—not forgetting the numerology and astrology of the inimitable Bejan Daruwala, with whom I kept up a lively correspondence.... Some of them, like Krishan Chander, enjoyed writing to me, and I was soon doing almost as much letter-writing as editing.

Another lively correspondent at the time was Padmaja Naidu, daughter of the poet-politician Sarojini Naidu. She was in charge of the Nehru Memorial Fund at Teen Murti Marg in New Delhi. The fund had commissioned me to write a children's biography of Jawaharlal Nehru, and for this I had to spend a few days in Delhi, going through Nehru's correspondence and fascinating jail dairies, which had been put at my disposal. Padmaja Naidu had me over for tea on two or three occasions. She was a lovely person, full of good non-political conversation, and we found our literary tastes coinciding—Hugh Walpole and J. B. Priestley being among our favourite authors.

It was ironical, that while I was writing my modest Nehru biography, I should be arrested on a charge of 'obscenity'.

I had written a story called 'The Sensualist', admittedly a partial exercise in the erotic, and it had been published in *Debonair*, India's answer to *Playboy*. A month later a policeman from Bombay turned up at the cottage with a non-bailable warrant for my arrest.

Consternation on the hillside. Children's author Ruskin Bond taken to the courthouse. Did it have to do something with the Emergency? Speculation was rife. But thanks to local goodwill and an enterprising lawyer, Mr Jain, the warrant was changed to a bailable one, and two months later I appeared in a court in Bombay to face the charge of 'obscenity' as defined in one of our archaic colonial laws.

The case dragged on for a couple of years, during which the prosecutor died, and witnesses failed to turn up. I had to put in a couple of appearances before I was finally given an honourable acquittal. I can't say I enjoyed the experience. I was quite friendless in Bombay, and *Imprint* did not want to be involved in a case concerning a rival publication. Only two writers came forward to speak on my behalf—the poet Nissim Ezekiel and the Marathi playwright Vijay Tendulkar. Others, when asked, backed off, and I don't blame them. Respectable people stay away from the criminal courts as far as possible.

With the Emergency over, R. V. Pandit came back to India and I relinquished my job with *Imprint*. He wanted me to work in Bombay and I was reluctant to abandon my perch in the mountains. And besides, after the case, my feelings for the big city were mixed. Somehow, I felt safer, more secure, in the protective fields of Pari Tibba and the surrounding hills.

However, I still had the telephone which had been installed for the purpose of conducting midnight calls with Mr Pandit. I never did care for the telephone (and even today I do without a cell phone) but I kept it for some time because it was a boon to some of my neighbours. Telephones were rare on the hillside, the only other one being the office phone up at the school. People were always dropping in to use mine. A hippie contacted his parents in Australia, asking for money; it took several hours to get through, and he forgot to pay for the call. Young men, or sometimes girls, needed the phone to arrange meetings or parties. The local midwife had given my number to all her patients, with the result that I was often awakened in the middle of the night, by an anxious relative urging me to send for the midwife as a baby was on its way. Prem or I would have to trudge halfway down to Barlowganj to fetch the lady. My assistance (at a distance) in all these confinements brought me goodwill from neighbours on the hillside.

The town had an old library where sometimes I pottered about, discovering or rediscovering forgotten authors—Nigel Balchin (*The Small Back Room*), Patrick Hamilton ('Hangover Square'), H. De Vere Stacpoole ('The River of Stars'), John Buchan, Lord Dunsany, Hugh Walpole ('Mr Perrin and Mr Trail'), among many deserving of an afterlife. The library itself was usually deserted, having some twenty or so members, and I liked to linger there, engaging in the solitude and the

The Hill of Enchantment

musty smell of old books.

We had a bookshop too, the Cambridge Book Depot, and I would drop in quite often to pick up the latest Ross Macdonald or Rex Street (I loved detective stories). Sometimes a Graham Greene or an Anthony Powell, or even a classic of travel, Mark Twain's *Life on the Mississippi* or Wilfred Thesiger's *The Marsh Arabs*. Over the years, my appetite for reading has never diminished. Books have been a source of delight, and I must have read close to ten thousand. Sometimes I think I'm a reader first and a writer second. Well, I never would have been a writer if books had not been an important part of my growing years. The library can still be seen, looking rather forlorn because it has no readers.

The easy tenor of our lives was shattered by a number of explosions on the hillside. Fragments of rock rattled on our old tin roof. The Public Works Department had arrived in force, building a new road, a so-called bypass around the mountain. And the cottage stood in its way. The road went straight through the property, taking with it our little patch of forest. Oaks, maples, pines, and our precious walnut tree were all bulldozed out of existence. Birds and beasts fled to Pari Tibba, still untouched. Part of our kitchen collapsed due to the reverberations from the blasting. The building remained, standing alone on the ravaged hillside.

It was a depressing time, made worse by the loss of Rakesh's infant brother to tetanus. His cries haunted us for days. We buried him near the stream, where small children were buried. I visited my secret pine knoll for the last time, and felt I would not see that mountain stream again.

Chapter 6

We took a flat in the town, close to The Mall, but the world was too much with us, and after a year we moved higher up the mountain to Landour, most of it a cantonment area with only a few dwellings.

I rented part of Prospect Point, a handsome old villa on the summit. Upper Landour had a beautiful walk around the mountain, views of the eternal snows, deodar forests, horse chestnuts, and quaint tea shops. But I never felt settled there, never felt at home. It had once been the stronghold of American missionaries, and their influence still prevailed, although most of the residents were now transient hippies or retired air marshals and brigadiers writing their memoirs. Somehow I fell out of place—not respectable enough for the old koe-kais, and too respectable for the hippies.

I did not get through much writing up there. My immediate neighbour, a French hippie, was learning to play the sitar, and practised all night, night after night, even when a forest fire threatened to surround the building. Her partner was an acupressure practitioner. He attempted to cure me of writer's cramps and almost broke one of my fingers. Late one night, retreating to his own quarters, he tumbled down the steep hillside and ended up in hospital with a broken leg. Acupressure had its limitations.

Our landlord (who did not really own the house) was constantly making difficulties for us. When some accommodation became available lower down the hill, I was happy to leave the heights of upper Landour for its lower reaches, just above the bazaar.

Here, at one end of Ivy Cottage, we found a permanent home.

The building—dating from the 1870s—was in a bit of a shambles, and the steps to our rooms were in a broken and dangerous condition. But there were twenty-two of them—the same as to my little barsati in 1951, my 'room on the roof', so I took them as a good omen. The windows were intact but ill-fitting, letting in a cold wind. And as the house was facing east, very

The Hill of Enchantment

exposed, it was always windy. Then the tin roof was rusty, worn through in parts, and leaking badly. We spent what we could on repairs and moved in hoping for the best.

The best was some time in coming, but I found I could work quite well in the room I had chosen to occupy—a narrow veranda that had been closed in by a single brick wall. We were on the second floor, and it gave me a view of the road below, and another road below it, several footpaths, a cluster of houses, a corner of Landour Bazaar, and in the distance rolling hills. Directly in one's peripheral vision was the Doon Valley stretching out between the Shivaliks and the Himalayan foothills. An infinite panorama which put me, almost literally, on top of the world. I couldn't help experiencing a sense of uplift.

And as a further omen of things to come, there, right before me, perhaps a mile as the crow flies, was Pari Tibba, my hill of fairies. And I was still able to climb its slopes covered in spring with irises, sorrel, daisies, and buttercups.

I set to work. Julia MacRae, who had been my editor at Hamish Hamilton, had started her own company—a small firm run by three or four women. They were

specializing in children's books and books on music. I wrote several stories for their Blackbird and Redwing series—'Cherry Tree', 'Getting Granny's Glasses', 'Ghost Trouble', 'Snake Trouble', 'Earthquake', 'Eyes of the Eagle', 'Dust on the Mountain'—and they duly appeared separately in hardcovers and were generally well received. Later, Rupa Publications bought the India rights and gradually the stories found their way into the hearts of many young readers across India.

But other good publications were disappearing. The *Illustrated Weekly* closed down, ending a historic chapter in literary journalism. Many good writers had seen their works serialized in that magazine, especially during the Mandy years: Kamal Markandaya, Bhaban Bhattacharya, R. K. Narayan, Ruth Prawer Jhabvala, T. H. White, Ahmed Ali, Aubrey Menen—but it had changed radically in recent years, losing its old readership without winning new readers.

Blackwood's too, closed down after some 200 years of great travel writing. It had reached its peak when the British empire was at its zenith, and now it faded away in much the same way, without any fanfare.

The *Christian Science Monitor* had also changed. From being a full-fledged daily newspaper, and an influential one at that, it had been reduced to a skimpy weekend tabloid.

In India, book publishing was still in its infancy, apart from textbook publishing for schools and colleges. This meant that Indian writers were forced to look abroad to be published—and this wasn't easy without agents or a prior reputation.

The Room on the Roof had been out of print for some time. Unavailable, that is, as Wilco had several hundred copies of its paperback locked away in a storeroom and conveniently forgotten. Along came an enterprising publisher of school books, Devendra Sharma of Students Stores, who operated from Delhi's Kashmere Gate. Armed with an old copy of my book, he took it to Mr A. E. T. Barrow, who ran the India School Certificate examinations, and persuaded that great man to have it prescribed as a text for students during this exam. First Mr Sharma had to buy up what was left of the Wilco edition; then he set about printing a plain brown paper-covered edition, made to look as unattractive as possible.... And it was used in schools for three or four years until Mr Barrow passed away. It brought me a few decent royalties, making life at Ivy Cottage a little more comfortable. And for that, I am forever grateful to Mr Devendra Sharma who passed away some years ago.

Still, even with some remittances from Julia MacRae in London, and some income from *The Room's* student edition and a few magazine stories, my income from writing (and this was now my only income) was barely taxable; just enough to meet our daily expenses, home repairs, Rakesh's school fees, and my indulgence in books and the occasional bottle of Rosa XXX Rum. The rum had to be denied when I went into the hospital with a duodenal ulcer. This was followed by surgery for piles, an operation that was bungled. I was almost two months in our small mission hospital, making a slow recovery from an infection and feeling depressed, as I felt I was going nowhere and achieving nothing. Then came a letter from David Davidar who was just setting up the Penguin office in New Delhi. He wanted to bring out a new edition of *The Room* as a Penguin paperback. I came to life immediately. There's nothing like good news to make you feel better, and recovery was rapid. Mind certainly influences matter, if given a chance.

Chance gives, and takes away, and gives again.

This was 1986, and I was fifty-two. Tumbledown

Ivy Cottage was proving lucky, and I would never be out of print again.

The Room, in its new avatar, did well, and was followed with several collections of stories—*The Night Train at Deoli*, *Time Stops at Shamli*, others—those stories that had appeared in magazines and papers here and abroad between 1955 and 1985; a couple of hundred at least. And my nature essays—mostly those that had appeared in the *Monitor*—reappeared in *Rain in the Mountains* and other collections.

At the same time, Mr Rajan Mehra of Rupa had acquired the India rights to some of the children's books published by Hamish Hamilton and Julie MacRae. The bad news was that Julia MacRae's small firm had closed down, with some of the titles going to other publishers, after which they gradually disappeared. Fortunately, the Indian editions took off and grew more popular over the years. Mr Mehra and his son Kapish have been good to me for some thirty-five years. Mr Mehra has a quirky sense of humour. After attending a literary event in Kathmandu, he took me for a flight over Everest in a plane that wobbled about alarmingly, as though determined to come down on the nearest mountain peak.

'You have to do a book a month for us, Mr Bond,' said Mr Mehra. 'Otherwise I'm opening the emergency door!' As the said door was right next to me, I promised to do my best. He spurred me on to do some humour writing, *Roads to Mussoorie* and *Funny Side Up*, among many other titles. Whenever he visits his Dehradun home, he sends me a potted plant from his garden. Potted poinsettias and geraniums vie for space with hundreds of books that I have accumulated over the years.

Looking back, I think I have been fortunate in having well-disposed publishers. There was C. R. Mandy when I started out. There was Diana Athill in London, and Kaye Webb when I did an early Puffin and wrote for *Puffin Post*. There was G. D. Blackwood (the magazine had always remained in the family). There was Devendra Sharma. Then David Davidar, who now publishes me under the banner of Aleph. There were others at Penguin. And there is the Mehra family and Rupa—a publisher that sends me a royalty statement on the first of every month! What more could a writer ask for?

Publishing in India has taken great strides since I set out on my literary journey in the 1950s. Now Indian writers can be published here and make a reputation for themselves (and some money too) without having to look for literary agents in the UK or USA. I tried an agent once or twice, but I could never hit it off with any of them, as they were always wanting me to write for the 'market'. And I'm not a market writer. I do my own thing. I love writing and I'm happy if I please a few readers. Rewards and awards have come my way, and I'm grateful for them, but I have never sought them out.

Chapter 7

The advent of the twenty-first century brought in many changes in the literary scene, especially in India. The internet provided a forum for writers and publishers. Well-known writers were becoming faces, mini celebrities. Writing suddenly became a glamorous occupation. Non-writers wanted their byline on a book. Self-publishing took off. So did literary festivals.

The lit fest soon became a phenomenon, spreading like wildfire through cities and small towns, even schools and colleges. Everyone jumped on the bandwagon. There was money in it too—chiefly for the organizers. A certain kind of writer found it a useful platform for propagating his views. Politicians got into the act; you couldn't keep them away. Stand-up comedians and mind-readers and jugglers popped up at these events, all in the name of literature, English or otherwise. Willy-nilly I found myself becoming part of the literary circuit. It was fun at times. On the plane to Bhutan, I met a young magician who was thrilled to know that as a boy I had lived next door to the great Gogia Pasha, the 'gilly gilly' magician, and that I had played with the rabbits that he used for some of his tricks. (We had been Gogia Pasha's tenants during one of my stepfather's brief tenancies.) Also at the Bhutan festival Shashi Tharoor had given me an imitation of Bertie Wooster and other Wodehouse characters. And in Calcutta (Kolkata), I was taken to the historic Park Street cemetery, where I was expected to summon up ghosts of long-dead empire builders. True, I have written a few ghost stories, not because I believe in the supernatural, but more as a tribute to great writers like M. R. James and Oliver Onions who had perfected their skills in this genre. Oliver Onions! Such an intriguing name. And it was real, not a pseudonym.

Book signings were all the thing. At one event a fond mother brought her little boy to me and said, 'My son reads your book in school.'

'That's nice,' I said, flattered. 'And what's the name of the book?'

'*Tom Sawyer*,' he said smartly.

I signed Mark Twain in his autograph album.

Another child, a girl of eight or nine, threw a tantrum because she couldn't get Shakespeare's autograph.

'Shakespeare couldn't come today,' said Sunil Arora of Cambridge Book Depot. 'But you can have Mr Bond's autograph.'

'I don't want his silly autograph,' she said. 'I want Shakespeare's!' And she strode off in disgust.

I'm not sure if these lit fests really did anything for authors or publishers or booksellers. There were some second or third rung writers who turned up at all of them, hoping perhaps to go up another rung or two—and finding the next rung missing! Writing as a profession is a game of Snakes and Ladders.

Certainly, I did no work during these trips. Plenty of readings and interactive sessions, but no time for writing. There were cocktail parties too, all part of the festivities. For many they were the main attraction.

When I look back at the writers of the last century it's hard to think of any who were more popular than Agatha Christie, the mystery writer, and P. G. Wodehouse, the humourist. They outsold most others by the millions—and still do. But they weren't party people, they avoided personal publicity, and seldom appeared at public events. On a rare occasion when

Wodehouse attended a literary dinner the lady sitting next to him said, 'I'm so glad you came. I've always wanted to meet Edgar Wallace.' Wodehouse was at his happiest in the company of his wife and dachshunds. Somerset Maugham had a horror of literary get-togethers. Compton Mackenzie fled to his small island in the Hebrides (and he had another in the Channel) to get away from the literary crowd.

The greatest of writers often worked in solitude or isolation, either from choice or because there was no choice: Dostoevsky from a prison cell; Thoreau from the wilderness of Walden; Steveman from a remote island in the Pacific; Victor Hugo from his exile on the island of Guernsey (where I saw his study and desk, still carefully preserved); Emily Brontë and her sisters from a lonely parsonage on the Yorkshire moors; William Blake from a humble country cottage. Conrad wrote his first novel, *Almayer's Folly*, while he was still at sea, captain of a tramp steamer. Kipling did not write his *Jungle Books* in India; he wrote them in the solitude of a hamlet in Vermont, USA. John Clare wrote some of his loveliest poems from a mental asylum.

There is a time for all things, even the writing of poetry, and it will happen when it must.

Solitude helps, but it isn't easy to find. Sometimes we must work in the bedlam of the big city, like O. Henry or Damon Runyon or Ring Lardner in New York; or Maupassant or Balzac in Paris; or Dickens in London; or Graham Greene or Patrick Leigh Fermor in some remote corner of the world, among the unfamiliar. A superb storyteller, B. Traven, the author of *The Treasure of the Sierra Madre*, hid his true identity so well that till today no one is quite sure who he was. That's the wonderful thing about great literature—it encompasses the globe, it encompasses all humanity. Little known works survive, bestsellers are forgotten. The charm of the unexpected, the magical wand of the fairy, leads us on.

∫

I am just one small writer working from the top of a fairly big hill. I write because I can express myself better with the pen than with my faltering tongue. I write because I love words and what you can do with them. I write because I love this planet and all that's beautiful upon it, and because I want to record my impressions of it. I write because I was born to write.

The writing began when, as a small boy, I made those lists of things I liked—books, films, music, birds, flowers, and then went on to write about people—friends, familiars, loved ones. I wanted to capture their essence before their personalities escaped me. So they are not stories so much as character sketches, imperfect portraits. Perfection is not possible. Excellent is attainable. We strive for it, and in the process we might just come up with something worthwhile, something worth preserving.

Some poets are remembered just for one poem—Ralph Hodgson for 'Time, You Old Gypsy Man', Alfred Noyes for 'The Highwayman', Rupert Brooke for 'The Soldier', Eleanor Farjeon for 'Morning Has Broken'.

'I think that I shall never see a poem lovely as a tree,' wrote Joyce Kilmer, whose 'Trees' has probably been anthologized more than any other poem. But she wrote other poems too. So did all the poets I have mentioned. We must search their work for other jewels, the gold dust in their well-tilled earth, for no good writer has ever stopped at one poem, one song, one tale, one celebration of the gift of life.

The Great Librarian has given each of us a garden to cultivate, even if it is only in the mind. Sing your

The Hill of Enchantment

song then, but do not take from any man his song.

During the last two years, I have been confined more or less to my little patch, my desk, my window with its view of the winding roads and rolling hills. No writer should be without a window. No man or woman should be without a window. It is a requisite of both body and soul.

As a boy, I always wanted a window, even when we were moving from one house to another. From one I saw litchi trees; from another the little canal; from another a wild overgrown garden. Even in London I had my window looking out on plane trees or, at worst, an advertising hoarding. One bed-sitter gave me a view of a cemetery full of old, moss-covered graves, dusty reminders of our transitory presence on the planet. A window in Delhi gave me a view of a petrol pump, another place of transition. Every window presents a different view of the human comedy. At eighty-nine plus I am a connoisseur of windows.

It is not very large, my present window, but it takes in a wide perspective, a panorama of valley, hills, ascending mountains, winding roads, a footpath, a water pump, a little bazaar—and of course, clouds.

The cloud formations are always changing. Here

come the monsoon clouds, dark and forbidding. A wind springs up and I must close the window or the rain will sweep into the room, washing out my words on this writing pad. It won't matter. I will write them again. Next month the clouds will vanish and the blue skies will prevail. The sun will burst through my window and give new life to these ageing limbs. Fluffy white clouds will come and go. The hillsides will still be emerald green, the horse chestnuts falling, the last wildflowers blooming before winter sets in. The dark clouds will come again, bringing snow and sleet. The sky is forever changing.

∽

I stand before my window. Rakesh has gone down to the hospital with a tiffin carrier containing lunch for his ailing father, my old friend Prem. Beena is upstairs, drying clothes on the roof. Siddharth, Shrishti, Gautam are in their rooms, occupied with laptops and other fascinating inventions. For me, the magic is outside, no further than the window sill, where a jungle crow is tapping on my window, demanding some of my breakfast. I open the window and part with a buttered

toast. Friend crow thanks me with a squawk and takes off. There were many crows, mynas, sparrows, thrushes, finches, parrots on the hillside when we first came here. They come no more; the traffic has frightened them away. Only the old crow visits me from time to time. I honour old friends.

Facing me is Pari Tibba. It's still there and still giving me stories—'Song of the Forest' and 'The Enchanted Cottage' not long ago—and the birds and small creatures still have somewhere to go. And from my window, I can see the pine-knoll, that magic place where I found inspiration long ago. I'm still here too, old friend. Trees have been my friends from the beginning.

Pari Tibba, Fairy Hill.

Sometimes, at night, I see those flickering green lights. Gautam insists they are just phosphorescent rocks glowing in the dark.

To hell with phosphorescent rocks. I believe in fairies.

PART TWO

Life Is Sweet, Brother

Chapter 8

'Life is sweet, brother.... There's day and night, brother, both sweet things; sun, moon, and stars, all sweet things; there's likewise a wind on the heath.'

—*Lavengro*

The wind is on the heath, the wind on the hill, the wind from the sea, the wind that is never still.... It gave George Borrow *Lavengro*; it gave Emily Brontë *Wuthering Heights*; it gave Joseph Conrad *Youth* and *Typhoon*; it gave Herman Melville *Moby Dick*; it gave Jack London his tales from the South Pacific; it gave Robert Louis Stevenson *The Ebb-Tide*; it gave Kenneth Grahame *The Wind in the Willows*. All over the world the searching wind has brought forth words and wonderful tales and rhythms from poets and storytellers.

Sometimes the wind is playful, light, and breezy; it rustles in long grass and in the leaves of trees; it can be soft and warm, fondling the good earth. Sometimes, in summer, it brings in puffy white clouds. From my window I watch them sail harmlessly by. In winter the clouds are dark and forbidding. Thunder blossoms in the sky. Pari Tibba is lit up by flashes of lightning, and a little later the wind and the rain come roaring over the forest, over the rooftops, over the sleeping town, whistling and shrieking and blowing away loose tin roofs and hoardings, uprooting and felling old trees, bombarding the bazaar with hailstones larger than marbles.... And by morning, the wind has wandered on, the sun is out, the sky cloudless. There is just a zephyr to remind us of the storm.

The wind has many moods. It caresses us to remind us that we are alive. It makes the blood sing in our veins.

I made friends with the wind when I was eleven or twelve years old. Up to then I had taken it for granted, as most of us do.

I was sitting on a bench in a quiet corner of the playing field of my school in Shimla. I was on my own. My friends, my playmates, were kicking a football

The Hill of Enchantment

around. Always a dreamer, I was dreaming of faraway places and far-off things.

Suddenly a wind sprang up. It seemed to come from Tara Devi, across the steep divide that separated that mountain from ours.

The wind came across the valley and entered my soul.

For the first time in my life I felt a stirring that was both physical and mental—or spiritual, if you prefer that word. But 'spirituality' isn't a word that means anything to a schoolboy who is always hungry, one eye on his books and the other on the tuck shop. No, I was never 'spiritual'. But I felt different, I wanted to do something, climb five mountains or swim seven seas. The school boundary was limiting. But I had to do something.

I wrote a poem.

It was my first poem—or one of the first. It has been altered a bit over the years, but here it is, more or less as it was first written.

Listen!

Listen to the dawn wind in the trees,
Listen to the summer grass singing;
Listen to the time that's tripping by,

And the morning dew falling.
Listen to the moon as it climbs the sky,
Listen to the pebbles humming;
Listen to the mist in the trembling leaves,
And the silence calling.

Not a great poem, but as good as some in my school readers. And it was written by the wind.

A couple of my friends came by, asked me what I was doing, and I read the poem to them.

'How can pebbles sing?" asked Joginder. 'How can the grass sing?'

But Cyrus liked the poem. 'I can hear the moon singing.'

'Then there's something wrong with your ears. You should see a doctor.'

'My ears are better than yours,' said Cyril, who did have big ears. There was a scuffle, a good-natured one.

The discussion of my poem was interrupted by the ringing of the school bell, which hung from a stand that looked rather like a gibbet. It was the bell for supper and the end of the poetry session. That school bell ruled our lives. Clang, clang, clang! It got us up for early morning PT, for meals, for classes, for games, for going to bed, and for getting out of bed.

The Hill of Enchantment

Towards the end of the year, in the early hours or late at night, someone removed the bell and flung it down the hillside. For a day and a half, there was peace, perfect peace, just the silence of the mountains, with agitated teachers running about in confusion. The bell was eventually found lodged in a blackberry bush and restored to its rightful place.

For some time, I was suspected of being the culprit, as I was known to wander about after 'lights out'. But it transpired that the villain was a disgruntled cook who had been given notice because he had put salt instead of sugar in the headmaster's morning cup of tea. This was sacrilege, of course. But the cook had influence in the kitchen, and the entire kitchen staff went on strike. For two or three days some of the boys, including my friends and I, volunteered to help out, peeling potatoes, slicing onions (a tearful process), making porridge, frying eggs, washing dishes, handing out sausages. It was great fun.

Sausages! These were mysterious objects, especially during and after the war years. No one knew what went into them. They were called 'sweet mysteries', after the famous song 'Ah! Sweet mystery of life'.

But to return to the wind that I experienced that

semester from time to time, especially when I was out on the playing field. It helped me score a few goals! I called it my 'adventure wind'. Just a light breeze usually, carrying with it the scent of pine needles and chestnut blossom. Perhaps it was the scent of the wind that inspired me—all those fragrances that it picked up on its way over hill and forest and mountain stream. For the pure mountain air is full of fragrance, and the wind will pick it up and carry it over five mountains and seven seas.

∽

When I came home to Dehra, in the Doon Valley, it was there too, although not so frequent, for the wind prefers the mountain to the valley.

In Dehra during my winter holidays, I became a walking person. This was in response to the emptiness of my home life, the lack of companionship, and the hectic social life of my mother and stepfather—parties and 'shikar'. I was usually left to my own devices....

My sturdy legs took me all over the town—a small town in the 1940s, with a population of 40,000 souls—into the bazaars, railway yards, bus stops, cantonment, and out to the tea gardens and sugar cane fields. Sometimes I sang marching songs:

Tramp, tramp, tramp along the highway
Tramp, tramp, tramp, the road is free!

(That was Nelson Eddy in *Naughty Marietta*.)

And there was 'Keep right on to the end of the road', made famous by Harry Lauder, Scotland's iconic music-hall entertainer.

It was seldom that I had a particular destination in mind, but sometimes my feet would take me to my grandmother's house on the Old Survey Road. Granny was a taciturn old lady who believed that little boys should speak only when spoken to. I found her tenant, Miss Kellner, more interesting.

Miss Kellner was a cripple; she'd been crippled since childhood when she'd fallen out of a horse-drawn carriage in Calcutta. Her arms and legs were crooked, her back was humped, and she held a pen with difficulty. She had servants who carried her about in an armchair. I don't know if she had relatives; I never saw them. But she seemed to be reasonably well-off and did not want for anything. I enjoyed talking to her, and she seemed to enjoy my company. She taught me to play simple card games and lent me her *Daily Mirror*, sent to her from London. This paper was full of scandals involving famous people, and Miss Kellner followed them avidly. I liked the paper for its cartoon strips (*Popeye* being one of them) and for its news about films and musical shows. But our conversations sometimes rose above the trivial.

'The good Lord gave us five senses,' said Miss Kellner one day. 'Do you know what they are?'

'Yes, of course. There's the sense of sight, the sense of hearing, the sense of smell, the sense of taste, and the sense of touch.'

'Good boy. And do you use them to the fullest?'

'I think so. I haven't really thought about it very much.'

'You take them for granted. So do most people. But if you really want to make something of your life, and get something out of it, you must use your five senses all the time. Look and learn. Listen! Do you listen?'

'Yes, Miss Kellner, I'm listening to you.'

'And what do you smell?'

'I smell something nice cooking in your kitchen.'

'Greedy boy. Don't you smell the flowers in your grandmother's garden?'

The Hill of Enchantment

'Yes,' I said. 'I like flowers that have a fragrance—roses, sweet peas, petunias, carnations....'

'And those without fragrance make up for it with their colour. Dahlias and zinnias! What's your favourite colour?'

'Lemon,' I said.

'Why so?'

'Because I like your lemon tarts!'

Miss Kellner would erupt in peals of laughter. Her ayah would be sent to the kitchen for the lemon tarts. She had a weakness for lemon tarts, and I developed a weakness for *her* weakness. I'm still on the lookout for lemon tarts.

Before I left, I touched her crooked hand and twisted fingers.

'The sense of touch,' I said.

Yes, the sense of touch, perhaps the most important of them all. The touch of a loving hand.

∫

A year or two later, after two brief tenancies, we spent a winter in the house near the canal, where I tried to create a record of sorts by reading the Bible, the *Complete*

Works of William Shakespeare, most of Charles Dickens, and Miss Kellner's *Daily Mirror*, all in three months. The following year, when I came home for the holidays, I found that my mother and stepfather had separated (it was just for a year) and she had taken a job as the manager of an old rundown hotel called Green's.

Hardly anyone stayed there. Meals were not provided. There were about a dozen rooms in reasonably good condition. One room boy managed all of them. But there was a billiards room and a 'marker', and in the evening, people would sometimes step in for a game of billiards or snooker.

I was given a small room of my own in the hotel, my mother, brothers, and sister staying in a small cottage behind the main building. It was interesting to observe some of the hotel's guests, their comings and goings, their activities, troubles, truimphs sometimes, and tragedies. And many years later, in the 1990s, they were to turn up in stories such as 'The Bar that Time Forgot' (the billiard room), 'The Late Night Show' (the cinema next door), 'The Skeleton in the Cupboard' (an old scandal), 'At Green's Hotel' (a serial killer!), and others in a little collection called *Secrets*. Some of the guests were quite friendly. An Air Force officer on leave took me to the pictures every evening during his stay. Another guest, a former badminton champion, gave me lessons in the hotel's badminton court. The room boy disappeared with my pocket money, the billiard marker disappeared with the billiard cues and balls. A down-and-out Anglo-Indian lady stayed for a month but couldn't pay the bill. The owner of the hotel, a Sikh gentleman, waived payment and she moved to the railway station's waiting room where she stayed a month before disappearing.

If hotel rooms could speak, they would have great stories to tell. They have provided some fine writers with great books—Vicki Baum's *Grand Hotel* (filmed with Greta Garbo and John Barrymore), Norman Collins's *London Belongs to Me* (the story of a boarding house), George Orwell's *Down and Out in Paris and London* (a series of rundown lodging houses); Dickens's inns and taverns; O Henry's seedy city dwellings; Raymond Chandler's cheap little hotel rooms; Conrad's captains' cabins; Jack London's yachts; Dracula's castle....

Hotel rooms are sad, lonely places. They have witnessed the worst of human nature, transients everyone, concealing our faults and failures behind neutral doors, putting on a show for the world outside, and finally checking out and returning to the reality of the world outside.

Sometimes the sun breaks through.

We can't live without windows. A closed room stifles the soul. The jail authorities know that, and they make it their business to see that, if ever you leave those prison walls, you will be a shell of a man. They destroyed many writers and poets. The only one they couldn't destroy was Dostoevsky, he had too strong a spirit.

∫

When I finished school, my mother packed me off to the Channel Islands—beautiful bays and beaches, but the local character was overwhelmed by thousands of tourists: every summer tourists from sunless England, spending their holidays lying in the sun and trying to acquire a little colour.

I met no writers in Jersey. No readers either, although the public library did alleviate my homesickness by providing me with the works of Rabindranath Tagore, Rumer Godden, Mulk Raj Anand, Christine Weston, Edward Thompson, and some whose works were set in the Far East—Conrad, Somerset Maugham, Maurice

The Hill of Enchantment

Collis (*Siamese White*, *Trials in Burma*), Robert Payne; these writers kept me going while I dealt with rejection slips (for my stories) and critiques (or lack of them) from the publishers to whom I had submitted my first novel.

As I've said earlier, I went through three jobs during that year in Jersey and was resigning myself to a dreary future as an accounts clerk in the health department when my 'adventure' wind came to my rescue.

In the Channel Islands, we were used to gales and stormy weather, but my adventure wind was something different. It had lain dormant for some time, and indeed I had forgotten about it, when, late one evening, I strolled disconsolate along St. Helier's promenade—deserted on a winter evening—the wind of my desires caught up with me. It came in from the sea, riding on the waves of a high tide, and crashing against the sea wall with an explosion of wind and water. The salt spray stung my face, my cap flew away, and I was hard put to it to keep up my balance, to stand up against the force of the wind. There was something personal about it. It was angry with me, it wanted to punish me for being weak-spirited and defeatist. I fought against it at first, turned homewards, but it would not let me go. So, I turned and stood against it, and accompanied it

to the pier, and stood there looking at the sea pounding against the sea wall and I said to myself, 'Calm down, I'm on my way. I'll leave tomorrow. I'll go to London and won't leave the city until I have a publisher for my book. I'm on my way!'

And the next day I threw up my job, said goodbye to my aunt and uncle, and took the little steamer to Southampton.

Chapter 9

'I'm on my way!'

It's a great song, the highlight of the all-Black operetta *Porgy and Bess*, the first major theatrical show that I saw in London. And it became my theme song. I'm still singing it today, seventy years later. Even if you can't sing very well, it's good to have a song to keep you going. That, and the wind behind you.

I have written elsewhere of my two years in London, and my return to India. I'd been back in Dehra for over a year before the book was published. And before I saw the book, there was a letter from C. R. Mandy informing me that it was going to be serialized in the *Illustrated Weekly of India*. That gave it a showcase in India. Illustrations by the great Mario Miranda added to its appeal. I followed the serialization with my young friends, and we had many a spicy party at Dehra's Chaat Corner. Copies of the book arrived as anti-climax, followed by a few pleasing reviews in the *New Statesman, The Scotsman,* and the *San Francisco Chronicle,* along with a couple of grumpy ones by critics who felt that someone just out of his teens had no business getting a novel published. John Wain in *The Observer,* said I wrote 'Babu English'. Perhaps I still do.

The Room on the Roof did not sell very well, and a year later, to my disappointment, it was 'remaindered'— that is, unsold copies were offered to the trade at a throwaway price. Mandy had already serialized a sequel, *Vagrants in the Valley* (again with Mario's illustrations), but André Deutsch wasn't interested in doing another book of mine, and my *Vagrants* went nowhere. Oddly enough, the German translation of *The Room on the Roof* (entitled *Die Strasse Zum Bazar*) did quite well and went into a club edition illustrated with some impressionistic line drawings. I had a copy for many years until it was 'borrowed' by a forgetful publisher friend, and never returned.

The Room hadn't really taken off, but I was turning out stories and articles at a good rate, and the cheques were coming in. The sums weren't large but they kept the jackals from my door.

At times I felt a little restless, dissatisfied. Dehra wasn't a very exciting place to live in, back in the 1950s. Our little Odeon cinema did not compare with the Odeon at Marble Arch, and the Chaat Corner wasn't Hyde Park Corner, although infinitely more respectable. But I had no regrets. I felt no desire to return to the dreary bed-sitting rooms of London. My rooms in Dehra were bright and airy, and there was no one to object if a friend or friends sometimes stayed with me. At times I thought of myself as a failed writer, but that did not stop me from writing—or from looking for something to write about.

I had a friend called Joshi, a college student, whose home was in a village in the hills, a day's march from Lansdowne, the recruiting centre for the Garhwal Rifles, a regiment that had distinguished itself in two World Wars.

The Hill of Enchantment

Joshi, a sturdy fellow destined for the army, invited me to accompany him to his village and stay with him for a fortnight. The prospect of living in a remote mountain village appealed to me; I had been a city dweller for too long, and I had a romantic notion of rural life.

Roads into the hills were few in those days, and to get to Lansdowne we had to first take the train to Laksar, across the Ganga; change trains and take another to Najibabad in the Terai; change again, and take a train to Kotdwar, a little town in the foothills. From Kotdwar it was a two-hour bus ride up to Lansdowne at a little over 6,000 feet. A very complicated journey, although the distance, as the crow flies, was not very great.

Joshi's village was a twenty-mile trek from Lansdowne. It was a footpath all the way. We set off early in the morning, hoping to reach his village by evening. It was May, hot and dusty. My 'adventure' wind stayed away. We plodded along, up one hill and down another and up again. '*Tramp, tramp, tramp, along the winding way....*' But I was too tired to sing. Just keeping up with Joshi was an effort. There were a couple of springs where we refreshed ourselves, but there were no shops, no dwellings, and we hadn't brought any food along. Joshi said we'd eat when we reached his village—and that seemed to be two or three ranges away!

I was about to collapse from hunger when along came a farmer on his way to Lansdowne. He offered to share his meal with us—thick rotis made from maize flour, along with a number of onions. I consumed most of his lunch. Never had onions tasted so sweet! Never have I relished a meal as much as I did that day. It made me a champion of the lowly onion. Better than an apple, it keeps those doctors away.

Onion refreshed, energy renewed, I covered the remaining distance without too much difficulty. Joshi's mother gave me a glass of milk. There were to be many glasses of milk during my stay, and I forbore to say that I hated milk—I was old-fashioned enough to avoid giving offence. We slept in the open courtyard. There was a lime tree near my cot, and its blossoms gave out a sweet fragrance.

We were about ten days in the village, or rather, above the village, as Joshi's family, being the most affluent, owned the most land on the slopes above the Nayar River. But there was no arrangement for one's natural body functions. I had to get up as early as possible, scramble up the hillside, and find a bush behind which I could evacuate my bowels in some privacy. I was never quite alone. Sometimes a large lizard would watch me from an adjoining rock. Although it never moved, I found it rather disconcerting. And sometimes a monkey watched me from the branch of a wild plum tree, making a mocking gesture and a rude noise, as though determined to establish its relationship with the human species.

Fortunately, after a few days of drinking milk by the bucket, I was constipated and remained so for the rest of my stay. I was none the worse for it. I enjoyed bathing in the river. I watched the children at play—and they stared at me with curiosity. With my sand-coloured hair, sunburnt face, and khaki shorts, I must have been an odd-looking alien. The children were very poor. All of them went barefoot. They were undernourished. It would be years before a road came to the village, bringing with it a little prosperity.

I found myself wishing I had brought something along to read. A book lover separated from books is a sad state of affairs. The only book in Joshi's home was a physics textbook. I shuddered at the sight of it. Not my favourite subject!

I am not a fussy eater, but I was getting tired of milk, beans and potatoes, and kheer (rice pudding, with more milk). After another long walk, I returned to my writing desk in Dehra with some enthusiasm. I got back to my room late at night; and the following morning, as soon as the restaurants opened, I dashed across the road to Kwality and treated myself to a breakfast of ham and eggs.

Chapter 10

'Life is sweet, brother....'

And so it was, most of the time. Although I loved reading *Walden*, I was no Thoreau. I was a failed novelist and a failed recluse. I had no intention of living on berries and wild honey, assuming they could be found in the wild. Fountains of milk were not for me. I was a comfort-loving dropout; I think that describes me quite accurately. But I could and would write. What else could give my life some meaning?

My two years of freelancing from Dehra passed quickly. I am lazy by nature and seldom sit at my desk for more than half an hour at a time. Even so, I turned out three or four stories and a couple of articles every month and communicated by post with editors and publishers. An air letter to the UK took about a week to be delivered; a letter to Bombay got there in two days. This was a good deal quicker than it is today. Most payments were made by cheque, hence the old saying, 'The cheque is in the mail'. It usually was, but the banks took ages to credit the money to one's account. Small payments came by money order, the postman handing over some crisp new notes. I loved those money orders. Receiving money from the postman and keeping on good terms with him (he could hold back a money order if he wanted) was less humiliating than going to the bank and asking the cashier if there was anything in my account before making a withdrawal. There was a certain bank clerk, a sweet-voiced acid-tongued cashier, who always greeted my arrival with enthusiasm, calling out for everyone to hear: 'Hello, Mr Bond, how nice to see you! Have you come to replenish your account?' I wanted to strangle him. But I should have known that there are no secrets in small towns. At best, I could get ₹50 for a story in the *Illustrated Weekly*. *The Statesman* gave me thirty-five. BBC Radio gave me £12 for a fifteen-minute story. And so, in a good month, I made about ₹300. I paid ₹30 for my two rooms, sixty for two meals a day at a nearby dhaba, and a fair amount for postage and stationery. I'd buy a book, go to the cinema, and share a few beers with friends and familiars. When I transferred myself from Dehra to New Delhi, I had about ₹500 in my savings account. The bank clerk smiled knowingly as I made my last withdrawal.

Always ready to take on a job, any odd job, when the going got tough, I found a lifeline with CARE, the American relief agency, which was just beginning to expand its self-help programme in India, with the blessings of the Indian government.

I have mentioned my small but interesting participation in Tibetan refugee resettlement. There were other projects too. I know nothing about farming but I was assigned to work with the Young Farmers Association in the Punjab. CARE was giving away steel ploughs to Indian farmers, and our director was photographed presenting one to Indira Gandhi, then helping her father Jawaharlal Nehru in various ways. But the steel plough did not find favour with farmers, young or old, who much preferred the traditional wooden plough, which was heavier and bit deeper into the soil, while the lighter steel plough bounced off the hardened ground. The plains of Punjab and the prairies of America are obviously made differently.

However, the gesture was appreciated and I made

several trips into rural Punjab, on one occasion buying a buffalo at an agricultural fair, as a 'gift from the people of the USA to the people of India'—as though we didn't have enough buffaloes! I was told by a bearded sage that a buffalo with blue eyes gave more milk than buffaloes with grey eyes, and I acted on this assumption, only to discover later that the old farmer had been pulling my leg. No harm done. And as you know, I never did care for milk, whether goat's, cow's, or buffalo's.

I went to small rural and mandi towns such as Moga, Rupar, Sangrur, Pathankot, sometimes travelling by bus, sometimes by jeep. A composite of these towns became the Pipalnagar of a short novel. It began as a sketch or short story. I'd met Khushwant Singh, always affable, always helpful, and he'd invited me to write something for *Yojana*, the magazine of the Five-year Plan, which he was then editing. My story had very little to do with Five-year Plans, but he published it, possibly out of a sense of mischief. It created no ripples, but I expanded it under the title 'Bus Stop, Pipalnagar'. It appeared in an American literary magazine called *New Renaissance*. Then it grew a little more and in time became the novella *Delhi Is Not Far*, which was published twenty years later. This writing record was

broken by 'Time Stops at Shamli', a long short story which took thirty years to get into print. It must be remembered that although there was a magazine market in India, there were as yet no publishers of fiction and general literature. Indian authors had to look abroad for publishers, and only a few broke the barrier. How different it is today!

Back in the CARE office in New Delhi, I fell out with the 'boss', a new director who was aloof and 'presidential' as compared to his predecessor. It wasn't failed ploughs or blue-eyed buffaloes that led to an estrangement, but his obsession with publicity, both for CARE and for himself. I was doing a Sunday column for *Hindustan Times*—had been doing it for at least a year—called 'Random Reflections'. It was really a nature notebook with meditative articles. Our new 'boss' wanted me to introduce something about CARE into it from time to time. This was going a little too far, and in any case *Hindustan Times* would have none of it. We fell out over this, and I put in my resignation. At the back of my mind I'd been wanting to get back to writing full-time, and to doing it from a place of my choosing. Now I'd given myself a justification of sorts. My mother and stepfather were horrified—as they had been when I returned from England—but after four years in New Delhi I was wilting a bit, and my 'adventure wind' was noticeably absent.

I dreamt of pine-scented breezes and cascading mountain streams, and was determined to make another dream come true.

Chapter 11

It was important to have a garden. Maplewood, surrounded by oaks and Japanese maples (their young leaves, not their mature leaves, in bursts of red), was built on the ledge of a steep hillside. This ledge was about the size of a badminton court and nothing much grew on it except grass and wild daisies. I'd grown up in the spacious lawns of the Jamnagar palaces, and then in my grandmother's Dehradun bungalow with its flower garden so beautifully maintained by Dhuki, our old gardener, who also found his way into some of my stories. (In *A Job Well Done*, he helps a small boy get rid of an unwanted guest.) I loved flowers—the fresh-faced cosmos, fragrant sweet peas, delicate petunias, upright hollyhocks, bold sunflowers, scarlet poppies, sturdy snapdragons…. But from the time I had left India to the time of my return and my sojourn in New Delhi,

The Hill of Enchantment

I had been starved of flowers and gardens. My home in London, my rooms in Dehra and Delhi had been without any space for growing things. Now that I had a little space to myself I wanted to do something with it.

Growing a plant is rather like writing a story. You plant a seed, you watch it sprout, you tend to it as it grows, you nourish it with loving care; and the flower, the fruit, is the climax of the story. And just as one story will lead to another, one plant will give you many more.

But the ground near the cottage was stony, hard, unyielding. Neither a steel plough nor a wooden plough would have been of any use. So, I thought, if I can't have a formal garden why not a wild garden?

And a wild garden it became.

A dandelion is as pretty as any flower, and so is a wild aster growing in a retaining wall. I collected seeds from the flowers growing on Pari Tibba and from the banks of the stream below and scattered them all over the ledge. I made a small pond, lined it with moss and reeds from the stream. I put down cuttings of dog roses and blackberry bushes wherever there was a crack in the ground, and I planted the bulbs and of corms of wild ginger and irises. And then I waited for it to rain.

It was early summer and it did not rain for several

weeks. I rested from my labours and went back to my typewriter and started typing out *Adventures of Rusty*. It was the little portable I'd bought in Jersey. The letter 'b' had broken off and I could not get a replacement. 'B' is an important letter. I typed out the novella without the 'b', and then spent days laboriously filling in the missing letters, page after page. In due course, I bought a new typewriter, a handsome Olympia, but for several months I was filling in 'b's', and uttering curse words beginning with the same letter. There were many of them!

And then the monsoon rains arrived, and within a few days my wild garden sprang to life. Bare branches gave out new shoots, fresh grass sprang up, seeds became seedlings and seedlings became saplings, and the entire hillside was transformed from a dusty yellow to a verdant green. Beside my little pond ferns sprang up, among them my favourite, the delicate maidenhair.

One morning, as I surveyed my handiwork or rather nature's handiwork, I saw a praying mantis balancing on the stem of a bush, staring at me as though sizing me up for a possible meal. And the next day I saw a leaf insect. At first, I mistook it for a dead leaf. And then it moved quite gracefully, a living thing, one of nature's wonders, amazing in its perfection.

The Hill of Enchantment

An insect garden! My wild garden was soon an insect garden. Beetles large and small paid me a visit—bamboo beetles, rhino beetles, stag beetles, and small beetles so colourful that you could mistake them for precious stones—rubies and emeralds and sapphires and bloodstones. Dragonflies hovered over the pond, butterflies stole nectar from the wild dog roses.

I had made a garden, and I was writing poems and essays and stories. Friends came to stay with me. There were other visitors too. Visitors from the forest, the streams, my hill of fairies. Having as a child been a writer of lists, let me list some of my visitors.

Foxes (I wrote a poem about one of them.) A friendly bat. (He became a poem too.) Night birds. An owl, a nightjar.

A panic-stricken barking deer, probably fleeing from a leopard. I did not see the leopard. But I was to see one later and wrote several stories about leopards—beautiful, cunning, and rapacious.

Long-tailed langurs, leaping from tree to tree, never missing a leap or breaking a branch. Athletes of the forest.

Long-tailed magpies. Sunbirds. Golden orioles. Redstarts. When the redstarts arrive you know that

winter is just around the corner.

A beautiful green snake gliding about the garden in search of field rats flooded out of their holes during the rains.

Frogs. They were quiet during the day but were in good voice after dark, treating me to operatic arias.

I wasn't a recluse. I walked up to the town almost every second day, visiting the post office, banks, bookshops, Kwality restaurant, usually in that order. In time, I had Prem and his growing family for company. When Rakesh was five, he started attending nursery classes at St Clare's, the little convent school which had just opened further up the hill. Sometimes I would accompany him to the school or fetch him home. The nuns from Kerala were very sweet and gentle, unlike those at the convent where I had spent the first two years of my schooling.

The Maplewood years passed quickly—too quickly. And then we had to move, for reasons already described.

༄

The family grew. Rakesh married when he was eighteen, and his wife Beena took over running the home.

Siddharth, Shrishti, Gautam, were all born in this house. Soon our Ivy Cottage flat was bursting. Prem opened a small ration shop on the by-pass, in a house built by him on a small rocky outcrop.

My books were accumulating. Not just the ones I read, but also those I'd written. Finally, they were beginning to sell. No longer did I have to search for one of my books in a bookshop, lucky to find a copy tucked away beneath a pile of other writers' bestsellers. Now a selection of titles would be up front, on display. It had taken me thirty years to reach this stage. No overnight bestsellers. I have had to worm my way into the hearts and minds of readers. But those readers are the ultimate reward. Like the twelve-year-old who came up and said 'Sir, I love your stories. I'm going to be a writer too!' If I can help to bring about a love for the written word, that in itself would be a reward worthy of all my years of struggle.

There have been friendships and love affairs, but it is my love affair with the written word that has been long, lasting, permanent. 'I celebrate myself,' wrote Walt Whitman, using the written word to celebrate himself. All writers are egoists—it's their driving force. But for a change let us celebrate the Word, the printed word.

Like the wind, it has penetrated everywhere, bringing with it joy, knowledge, vistas of thought and freedom, the poetry of life, and the poem of all our days.

⁓

Dusk has fallen, and a full moon is coming up over Landour. At this distance it is certainly more beautiful, more inviting, than it is in those pictures of a dead and barren landscape that we see so often these days. Here we are, blessed with a planet full of green and growing things, magnificent mountains, forests, and rivers, birds of brilliant plumage, myriads of forms of life; but we choose to distance ourselves from it, to trample upon its generous nature, and reach out instead to an orb of lifeless granite. Maybe that's something out there that we can destroy too once we have finished decimating our own habitat.

The man in the moon meant something to a small child. The barren craters of the moon are a disappointment. The magic has gone. We will have to create a little magic of our own.

Night is coming on. The air is still, my 'adventure' wind is elsewhere. A few hundred yards away is the small hospital where Prem is fighting for his life. He has grown old with me. Last week the doctor said he had only two or three hours to live. The doctor did not know Prem—a stubborn, contrary fellow, inclined to do exactly the opposite of what was expected of him! This morning he woke up and demanded a hot samosa.

'Life is sweet, brother....'

We do not surrender it too easily.

Across the divide, I can see those little green lights twinkling on Pari Tibba, Fairy Hill, the hill that gave me so many stories.

They are coming closer!

In the still of the night, on the enchanted air, they are floating towards me.

They are fireflies. And just as good as fairies.

One of them settles on the windowsill, a little glow-worm sending out a beacon of hope, lighting up the darkness.

I put out the light, open the window.

And then the room is full of fireflies, there must be ten or more of them, floating gently here and there, bringing sweetness and light into the twilight of my life.

*Recommended Reading
by Ruskin Bond*

Some books about writing and the writing life

It's Me, O Lord! An Abstract & Brief Chronicle of Some of the Life with Some of the Opinions of A. E. Coppard by A. E. Coppard
The Summing Up by W. Somerset Maugham
A Writer's Notebook by W. Somerset Maugham
The Years with Ross by James Thurber
The Crack-up by F. Scott Fitzgerald
The Diary of Virginia Woolf
Walden; or, Life in the Woods, and the journals of Henry David Thoreau
The journals of André Gide
The journals of Arnold Bennett
A Fragment of Life by Arthur Machen
Literature and Labour: An Anthology of Effort edited by Richard Wilson (rare)
Margin Released: A Writer's Reminiscences And Reflections by J. B. Priestley
Performing Flea by P. G. Wodehouse
The Mirror of the Sea by Joseph Conrad

Present Indicative by Noël Coward
All the Books of My Life by Sheila Kaye-Smith
The Letters of J. R. Ackerley edited by Neville Braybrooke
Writers on Writing, edited by Walter Allen
Unknown Masterpieces: Writers Rediscover Literature's Hidden Classics edited by Edwin Frank (New York Review Books)

Some enchanting books on nature, wildlife, and the great outdoors

The Valley of Flowers by Frank Smythe
Romance of Plant Hunting by Frank Kingdon-Ward
Jungle Folk: Indian Natural History Sketches by Douglas Dewar
A Naturalist on the Prowl, or in the Jungle by EHA (E. H. Aitken)
The Tribes on My Frontier; an Indian Naturalist's Foreign Policy by EHA
A Nature Notebook by M. Krishnan
Sundials of the Seasons: A Selection of Outdoor Editorials from The New York Times by Hal Borland
Green Laurels: Lives and Achievements of the Great Naturalists by Donald Culross Peattie
Singing in the Wilderness: A Salute to John James Audubon by Donald Culross Peattie
The Story of My Heart by Richard Jefferies
The Gamekeeper at Home by Richard Jefferies
Walden by Henry David Thoreau
The Jungle in Sunlight and Shadow by F. W. Champion
Far Away and Long Ago: A Childhood in Argentina by W. H. Auden